Vegetable Gardening

A beginner's guide to vegetable gardening and growing delicious vegetables from home!

Table Of Contents

Introduction 1

Chapter 1: Essential Things Novice Gardeners Should Know 3

Chapter 2: Your Location and Frost Zones 10

Chapter 3: All About Companion Planting and Determining the Most Suitable Garden Type 15

Chapter 4: Flat Bed Garden 20

Chapter 5: Container Garden 22

Chapter 6: Vertical Garden 25

Chapter 7: Raised Bed Garden 27

Conclusion 29

Introduction

I want to thank you and congratulate you for downloading the book, "Vegetable Gardening".

This book contains helpful information about vegetable gardening, and how you can do it from home!

In this book you will learn about the different climate areas, and when it's suitable to plant vegetables in each particular zone.

You will discover how to properly prepare and maintain the soil for your garden, including how to balance the PH level, create and use compost, manage pests, and effectively use mulch and fertilizer.

You will also learn about the different gardening methods that you can use to grow vegetables. These include container gardening, companion planting, flat bed gardening, vertical gardening, and square foot gardening. This book will help you decide what suits you best depending on your available space, budget, and plants that you'd like to grow.

A list of vegetables that are suited to different climates and garden types is also provided. This will allow you to easily choose which plants to grow, and where you should plant them.

Overall, this book will explain to you tips and techniques that will allow you to successfully create your own vegetable garden with ease, no matter what climate you live in, or space you have available!

So let's get started, and begin to work on creating you an amazing vegetable garden today!

Thanks again for downloading this book, I hope you enjoy it!

Chapter 1:
Essential Things Novice Gardeners Should Know

Most commercial vegetable growers use pesticides and other chemicals to make their produce more appealing. They intend to entice buyers, such as you, to buy from them. Even if these growers claim that they only sell organic produce, you can never be sure whether they are telling the truth. The best way to ensure that you will be getting organic and chemical-free produce is to grow your own vegetables in your home garden.

It's not difficult to grow your own vegetables, although it could be challenging at first, especially if you are a complete novice in the world of gardening. Once you understand the basics of vegetable gardening, everything will be easier and you will be able to work comfortably in your garden.

In this chapter, you will learn the basic essentials that a gardener should know and have in order to grow the most succulent and appetizing produce possible.

Getting Acquainted with your Soil

The kind of soil to use depends on the type of garden that you would like to have. You can use garden soil, the soil that you have in your backyard, or soil media. You need to make sure that you are using healthy soil that is free from disease and pests. The ideal soil temperature should not drop below 70°F.

If you are going to use the soil in your backyard, then you need to remove the grass and weeds first. Using a shovel, metal rake, or hoe, you must loosen the soil to provide the needed aeration and drainage. You will also need to add fertilizer and compost to feed your plants with the right nutrients. You can buy fertilizer from garden centers, suppliers, or nurseries. You can also buy your compost from the mentioned providers, or alternatively make your own to save some money.

There are times when using potting mix is the safest and the most suitable option, especially if you are not sure if the soil outside your house is safe. Using contaminated soil in your garden will eventually kill your plants and all your efforts will be wasted. Be safe and be smart, and ensure that your soil is suitable. As mentioned earlier, there are certain types of garden that prefer a particular soil or media when growing vegetables; we will discuss them all later.

Giving the Right Amount of Light

Plants produce their food through a process called photosynthesis which is only possible if chlorophyll in plants can get adequate amounts of light. Although there are vegetables that prefer shady areas, they still need some light to grow.

There are also times when you may need to provide artificial lighting to your plants to compensate somewhat for the lack of the needed amount of sunlight.

In general, gardens that are facing south should expect the full glory of the sun the entire day provided that nothing blocks or stops the rays from penetrating your garden. Gardens that are facing north don't have access to direct sunlight and the presence of buildings, tall trees, and other things that can block the rays of the sun make it difficult for the plants to grow.

Choosing the Vegetables to Grow

The most suitable vegetables to grow depend on the type of garden that you have, and your choice of home vegetable garden depends on the kind of space or area that you have. Luckily, you can grow vegetables even if

a. you have a limited space;

b. your area does not have access to direct sunlight; or

c. you do not have ample time to spend on gardening.

You can also choose first the kind of vegetables to grow and decide on the kind of garden that suits your vegetables. It's also good to know the frost zones and last frost date to determine when it's the best time to start planting your vegetables in your particular area.

The Right Amount of Water and its Frequency

Water is also important in growing your vegetables. As a general rule, you need to water your garden at least three times a week and you may need to water more during hot days, but do not over water.

It is recommended that you water your plants during the parts of the day when it is cool, such as the early morning when the sun isn't at its highest, or in the afternoon when they temperature has dropped. The water will evaporate quickly if you water when the sun is at its hottest.

Compost

Compost can help the roots of your plants absorb moisture or water before it drains. Compost is also rich in disease fighting elements and provides essential nutrients to your plants in order for them to grow well. You don't need to use or add much fertilizer if you have compost in your soil. The trick is to put compost near the roots of the plants to provide the most benefit. You can also opt to put your compost on the surface, but it won't be as effective as when you incorporate it into the soil.

Fertilizer

Your vegetable garden will benefit a lot from regular application of fertilizer. Although chemical fertilizers are efficient and potent, using organic fertilizer is just as effective but has an added measure of safety for both you and your garden.

Your plants need potash, nitrogen, and phosphorus to grow, and fertilizers can provide such nutrients. However, be careful not to give too much or else it can lead to excess minerals. This excess usually occurs when using chemical fertilizers. The excess nutrients can be washed away by the rain or irrigation and contaminate the water sources being used by people and animals which in turn can cause health problems.

Consider using the following organic fertilizers:

1. Kelp Fertilizer

Fertilizers using kelp as a base contain potassium and a bit of nitrogen. Kelp has the ability to stimulate the development of your soil and help your vegetable garden yield more produce. It also helps your plants develop tolerance for temperature extremes such as cold and almost icy weather and prolonged exposure to sunlight.

2. Alfalfa Meal

This plant-based fertilizer may not contain the right amounts of phosphorus, potash, or nitrogen, but it can help to improve the quality of your soil and produce more nutrients for your vegetables to feed on. It is completely organic and you don't need to worry about the excess nutrients that may cause problems later on.

3. Animal Manure

Animal manure is also a good organic fertilizer. You can prepare such fertilizer yourself or you can buy some ready-made at garden supply stores. Applying fresh manure directly can burn your plants due to the high nitrogen content of the manure. You need to compost your fresh manure before you can use it as fertilizer.

Mulch

Mulch can hold moisture in and hinder the growth of weeds. After planting, spread mulch on top of the soil. Leave some space surrounding your plant and avoid mulching up against the stem to prevent rotting.

Mulch is available at garden supply stores (wood chips are the usual material) or you can make your own using leaf litter (without disease) and grass clippings.

If you are a novice gardener, it is always safe to start small and then expand later in the summer or next spring. Pull the weeds when you spot them, water regularly, fertilize during the growing season, and then sit back and enjoy the fruits (or vegetables) of your labor.

Basic Things that you Will Need to Make Work Easier:

Trowel or Shovel

A trowel is the most useful tool in gardening (or a shovel if you have wide areas to cover). It is useful for scooping, mixing, and transferring the soil from one area to the next. Your hands won't get too dirty and you can also use it if you need to transfer your plants.

Gloves and Apron

Wearing gloves while working in your garden can help protect your hands. Most gardeners prefer wearing gloves, although there are some who find it easier to tend to their garden with their bare hands. Many people also like to wear an apron while gardening to prevent dirt and stains from getting on their clothes.

Bubbler

A hose-end bubbler can help soften the flow of water and prevent soil washout during watering. You simply attach it at the end of your hose and water your plants as you normally would.

Watering Can

You can also use a watering can if you want to have better water flow control. It is also best to use it when watering your indoor plants.

Mister

A mister can be a simple hand spray which can provide extra humidity to your plants, especially the ones in containers. You can also use your hand spray to remove the dust on the leaves and make your plants look lively.

Pruning Shears

Every gardener must have pruning shears to cut off dead leaves and stems. The shears can also be handy during harvesting.

Wheelbarrow

A wheelbarrow is a great help whenever you need to transport your plants from one location to the other. You can also use it to help you carry things and avoid possible back injury.

There are some garden types that require other things to help make your work easier and make your garden survive under any condition. Just see to it that your tools and equipment are well maintained and protected as well as durable in order to serve you well and for a long time.

Before knowing the different garden types, it is wise to know first the different frost zones and locations that can help determine the best time to start planting and the kinds of vegetables to plant.

Chapter 2:
Your Location and Frost Zones

Planning your own vegetable garden is not difficult. Having a reliable vegetable garden planner as a guide can also help a lot. Aside from determining the right soil, you also need to know the best location, frost zones, and last frost dates to ensure the greatest yield possible.

Determining the Right Location

Your vegetable garden needs the right amount of sunlight; you need to choose a good location to make this possible. It is advisable to put your vegetable garden where it can catch the most sunlight, but know that there are some vegetables that are not fond of sunshine. It is also wise to choose a location where there is no heavy traffic, or where no one in your household will pass through your vegetable garden.

So where in your property is the good location for a vegetable garden? It should be a place that gets enough sunlight and far enough away from foot-traffic. An often good place is to have your vegetable garden near your property walls.

U.S. Frost Zones

Knowing the frost zones can help you calculate the best time to start planting your vegetables.

You will find the approximate last frost dates with corresponding temperature for the different zones below:

Zone A - Last frost date is approximately mid June with lowest temperature around 40° to 30° below zero.

Zone B - Last frost date is approximately early June with lowest temperature around 30° to 20° below zero.

Zone C - Last frost date is approximately late May with lowest temperature around 20° to 10° below zero.

Zone D - Last frost date is approximately mid May with lowest temperature around 10° below zero to 0°.

Zone E - Last frost date is approximately late April with lowest temperature around 0° to 10°.

Zone F - Last frost date is approximately early April with lowest temperature around 10° to 20°.

Zone G - Last frost date is approximately early March with lowest temperature around 20° to 30°.

Zone H - Last frost date is around February with lowest temperature around 30° to 40° or higher.

The given are only approximate dates. It is recommended to check your local weather forecasts regularly so as to come up with your best judgment regarding the matter.

Areas that belong to Zone A are the north western part of Wisconsin, upper half of Minnesota, northern part of North Dakota, north eastern part of Montana, some parts of upper Maine, and Wyoming's south western region.

Areas that belong to Zone B are most parts of Wyoming and Montana, lower half of Minnesota, the rest of North Dakota, the rest of Wisconsin, South Dakota, the rest of Maine, upper parts of New Hampshire and Vermont, and northern New York State.

Areas that belong to Zone C are Iowa, mid part of Idaho, most parts of Colorado, northern part of Pennsylvania, western parts of Montana, Nebraska, lower parts of Wisconsin, upper parts of Indiana and Illinois, the rest of New York State, most parts of Michigan, the lower part of Vermont and New Hampshire, the western side of Massachusetts, and southern Maine.

Areas that belong to Zone D are some parts of western and south eastern Colorado, the rest of Pennsylvania, more than half of Oregon (eastern side), Kentucky, northern Idaho, the rest of Massachusetts, the south western part of Idaho, the upper part of Texas, the eastern part of Washington, West Virginia, western Utah, the majority of Kansas and Missouri, Ohio, lower part of Illinois and Indiana, Connecticut, and Rhode Island.

Areas that belong to Zone E are the majority of Oklahoma, southern Washington, the mid part of New Mexico, western Nevada, the upper part of Arkansas, southern Utah, northern Arizona, Tennessee, northern Alabama and Georgia, the mid upper part of Texas, Virginia, northern Mississippi, and the western part of North Carolina.

Areas that belong to Zone F are the lower half of Arkansas, the western part of Washington and Oregon, the upper part of Louisiana, the mid lower part of Texas, South Carolina, the rest of Alabama and Georgia, the upper part of Florida, and the rest of Mississippi.

Areas that belong to Zone G are the mid part of Florida, the western and southern part of California, the lower part of Texas, and the south western part of Arizona.

Areas that belong to Zone H are some parts of California and Arizona, and the lower part of Florida.

Keep the guidelines handy and always check your local weather forecast for possible changes.

The Best Time to Plant

It is crucial to plant your seeds at the right time. The key is knowing when you will see the last frost in your area. Some vegetables taste more succulent after a bit of frost. Be careful not to plant your crops that are suited to warm season when the ground is still cold with some frost on it.

There are also packets of seeds that indicate the best time to plant them, and it is prudent to follow the writing on the packets. To give you an idea, see the following time guide to plant certain vegetables.

1. Before Early Spring

It is best to plant onions, peas, and spinach as soon as the ground is ready to be worked. These crops will taste more delicious when planted at such times.

2. Early Spring Crops

Early spring crops to start with are lettuce, cilantro, potatoes, kale, cabbage, beets, broccoli, carrots, dill, celery, radishes, and kale. These crops are easy to maintain and they are among the best crops for novice gardeners to begin with.

3. Crops that are Suitable to Plant After the Date of the Last Frost

Crops that belong in this section include cucumber, basil, eggplant, peppers, tomatoes, melons, beans, pumpkin, corn, and squash.

As a constant reminder, start with a small garden patch to see if you will be able to handle bigger areas without sacrificing anything in return. It's nice to have a vegetable garden which won't eat into your time too much!

Chapter 3:
All About Companion Planting and Determining the Most Suitable Garden Type

Did you know that there are also plants that can safeguard your vegetables from pests and other invaders? Well, there are and you can easily incorporate companion planting with your vegetable garden.

To tell you the truth, companion planting is not just about pest control. By combining the plants carefully, they can benefit from each other by way of providing the needed soil nutrients, attracting beneficial insects, posting as a decoy for pests, and giving a sort of shield against too much sun and wind.

Possible Plant Combinations to Try

French marigolds give off a strong odor that greenfly and blackfly find repulsive. The said pests usually attack tomatoes so it's best to plant some marigolds near your tomatoes to ward off these insects.

Carrots and leeks are good together and they will benefit a lot from each other. Carrots can ward off leek fly and leek moth while leeks can stop carrot fly invasion.

Sage is a wonderful herb and you can grow it together with carrots or other plants that belong to the cabbage family. Both have robust scents that can easily and effectively ward off each other's attackers or pests.

You can plant nasturtium together with cabbages to serve as a sacrificial lamb. Nasturtiums can serve as magnet to attract caterpillars to feed on them instead of your cabbage patch.

The trick here is to plant the companion plants at the same time as your target vegetable to prevent the pests from invading your patch.

Other Companion Plants to Try

Asparagus can prevent the minute nematodes from bringing trouble to your tomatoes. Nematodes usually attack the roots of tomatoes and will eventually cause the plants to wither and die.

Chervil can safeguard your lettuce against aphids.

The onion scent in chives can easily stop the aphids from approaching your sunflowers, chrysanthemums, and tomatoes.

Dill, on the other hand, does not stop any pests but attracts the insects that can stop the plant pests. It can attract hoverflies which eat aphids. It can also attract the beneficial predatory wasps.

Aphids can be a major headache, but not if you have coriander in your vegetable garden because it also helps repel aphids.

Tansy has a strong odor which deters ant invasion.

Yarrow can boost the vitality of other plants in your garden. It can also attract beneficial ladybirds and hoverflies to visit your garden.

Composting

You can use a homemade compost bin or make an open one in your yard; just make sure to put it where it won't bother anyone. An open composting site can attract rodents and other pests, but it is easier to maintain.

You can use an ordinary container with a lid as your compost bin. Drill some holes at the bottom and sides of the container. Add some dirt to your compost bin. Add some shredded newspaper or used paper next before adding the materials for composting.

You can throw in coffee grounds and filters, vegetable and fruit peelings, tea bags, eggshells, more newspaper scraps, fur, leaves, cardboard, hay, grass clippings, paper, shells of nuts, yard trimmings, hair, wood chips (sawdust included), dead plants (make sure they don't have any disease), lint, and ashes.

Be careful not to throw in lard, grease, and oil. You should not throw in dairy products such as milk, butter, yogurt, egg yolk, or egg white. Charcoal ash or coal, meat scraps, twigs or leaves of black walnut tree, and fish bones are also not to be included. It is likewise foolish to throw in plants with diseases, pet waste, and yard trimmings that were treated with chemicals.

You can also make an open composting area using four wooden poles and then wrap chicken wire around the poles. Secure the wire using a nail.

Mix or turn your compost once a week to provide good aeration. You should also add a scoop of new soil when necessary. Your compost will be ready in two to four weeks.

Care and Maintenance

Water your plants regularly and take note when the leaves suddenly change their color. It is possible that pests have invaded your plants and you need to check underneath the soil if you can't see anything above the soil. Remove the pests right away or remove the entire plant if you suspect that it has a disease.

If the leaves become darker than usual, then it is an indication that they need more light. Try transferring your plants to an area where they can get ample amounts of light.

If the leaves turn yellow even though you are watering them on a regular basis, then try watering them only occasionally until you see the color become normal again. The leaves will turn yellow due to over watering.

Feed your plants with fertilizer on a regular basis (once a month to once every three months will do) and add compost at least once a year.

Remove the weeds and pests immediately before they bring further problems.

Choosing the Type of Garden

There are certain types of garden that are most appropriate for the available space that you have, and the plants you'd like to grow. Having a small space does not mean that vegetable gardening is no longer possible and having a big space does not necessarily require you to start big.

The different types of vegetable garden to choose from are flat beds, container, verticals, and raised bed. Each type will be discussed in the succeeding chapters to help you decide which type is the most suitable for you.

Chapter 4:
Flat Bed Garden

If you have ample space for an outdoor vegetable garden, then you might want to try a flat bed type of garden. This type of garden provides you with almost limitless options of the kind of vegetables you can grow. You don't need to make much preparation before you can set up your vegetable garden. You don't need to construct anything except if you need a trellis for your vines.

Flat beds do not require you to go through a tedious preparation. All you really need is to prepare your soil prior to planting. It is also recommended to make clear divisions or sections by putting markings such as stones to separate one section from the other.

Soil Preparation

You need to clear your soil first by removing the dead crops, weeds, and rocks. You need to make preparations at least a week before your intended date of planting. Loosen the soil for a bit so it will be easier to plant your vegetables later on.

If you have poor soil in your backyard, then you need to amend it first before planting your vegetables. You can add compost and fertilizer. If you have acidic soil (you can check the pH balance of your soil using a test kit) you need to put in ground limestone. If you have alkaline soil, then you need to add pine sawdust.

If you have a perfectly balanced soil, then you only need to add compost and fertilizer before you can begin planting your vegetables.

Ideal Vegetables to Plant in Flat Beds

You can start with cucumber, eggplant, bush beans, broccoli, Swiss chard, potato, peas, lettuce, cauliflower, and squash. The mentioned vegetables are easy to grow.

Other Concerns

Animals that usually go underneath the ground can wreak havoc on your flat bed garden.

The most ideal vegetables for flat beds are those that need lots of space to grow or if they have roots that need to go deeper.

You can use pathways as dividers for your flat beds to prevent trampling on your vegetables. Placing a plastic cover over the paths can also prevent weeds from sprouting.

Chapter 5:
Container Garden

A container garden is best for those people with limited space or who do not own a backyard. You can grow just about anything in containers as you normally would in a regular backyard garden. You need to choose your containers carefully and should spend more time with your container garden than a conventional garden. You also need to make sure that your plants get the right amount of light, the containers have proper drainage, and your plants can get the right amount of nutrients.

Soil Preparation

The most suitable soil to use for container gardening is a potting mix of one part coir peat, one part vermiculite, and two parts compost. You can also buy a prepared potting mix from your local supplier.

You need to soak the coir peat in water to rehydrate it. The packed coir peat usually comes with instructions so be sure to carefully follow them. Mix the rehydrated coir peat and vermiculite together. Make sure to mix them well before adding your compost.

Containers to Choose

Large containers are great if you plan to grow large vegetables. Deep containers are suitable for vegetables that grow beneath the soil or have deep roots.

You can use any containers as long as they meet your purpose. You can even use recycled materials such as tin cans, old buckets, or jars. Just make sure to have enough holes to provide good drainage for your plants.

Some of the containers to choose form are terra cotta pots, barrels, wood containers (choose redwood or cedar), tin, and plastic.

When filling your containers with soil, leave one inch allowance between the rim of the container and the top level of your soil. Doing so can prevent soil washout when you water your plants. It is also recommended to use trays beneath the containers to catch the water.

Artificial Lighting

For containers that you intend to put in your house, you need to provide artificial lighting to meet the required amount of the needed light for your plants to produce their food.

In every 18" by 18" square, you need a 100-watts artificial light to aid your plants' food production. Alternatively, you can simply carry your containers outside when they require light.

Ideal Vegetables for Container Gardens

You can plant beans, okra, tomato, eggplant, cucumber, and herbs in containers. You can also try some carrots, beets, collard greens, spinach, broccoli, scallions, and cabbage. You can plant the same vegetables that you can grow in a flat bed, but you need to have more patience and diligence when maintaining a container garden.

You need to carefully determine the size of your plant when fully grown and prepare a container that will be able to accommodate your plant in its maximum growth. You may also need to transfer some of your plants to other containers once it gets crowded or they begin to outgrow the container.

Use of Neem Oil

If you have a container garden, then you can use neem oil to prevent plant disease. It can also be used as a natural pesticide. All you need to do is apply some oil on the leaves and stem of your plants. The oil is a natural fungicide and pesticide, and it can discourage insects from feeding and harming your plants.

If you suspect that a particular plant has a disease, you need to separate it from the rest of your plants because it may infect the others.

Container gardening may require a bit more time, but it's ideal if you have limited space.

Chapter 6:
Vertical Garden

A vertical garden is similar to a container garden, but a vertical garden is suitable for someone with even more limited space. Vertical gardens usually have pocket type containers that are mounted on a wall or a frame. Setting up such a garden may require more work than setting up a regular container garden.

You can mount as many containers as you want, but make sure that the number of pockets will not make your wall look awkward. You can even turn your vertical garden into an added interior décor while providing fresh produce. You should provide trays (or have a customized one that runs the length of your wall) at the bottom to catch the water whenever you water your plants.

You can also choose to assemble a movable frame to hold your pockets and just move it outside whenever you need sunlight for your plants. Most gardeners find this more convenient.

Some of the advantages of the vertical garden are that you only need to have a wall or frame where you can mount your containers, so it won't take up so much space. It can make your wall literally come alive, and you don't need to use too much water (some water will simply drip to the next pocket or container). If you have a movable frame, you can always take your plants outside to catch some sunshine, or simply keep your frame near a window.

You can plant the same types of vegetables as in a traditional container garden, but you may want to reconsider planting deep rooted ones or the ones that may require a large space to grow. The soil preparation is the same with the traditional container garden. Obviously, you can choose to have a vertical garden and a traditional container garden at the same time.

Some suggestions would be petite herbs with shallow roots and other vegetables that don't need a large space to grow. You can try oregano, thyme, basil, sage, and spinach.

A lack of space should not stop you from having a vegetable garden. Container gardening and vertical gardening can be your best ally in achieving your purpose of having fresh produce even if you have limited space.

Chapter 7:
Raised Bed Garden

Most vegetable growers find raised bed gardens to be the most suitable option. It is a combination of a container garden and a flat-bed garden. A raised bed is best if you have plenty of space in your backyard or your property.

Assembling your Raised Bed

Most gardeners love this type of garden because they have better soil control, weed control, and easier access. You don't need to bend too far to access your garden, so it's perfect if you don't have amazing mobility.

You can use untreated wood, bricks, cinder blocks, and rocks for making the frame for your raised bed. The usual height of a raised bed is six inches, but there are some who prefer their raised bed to have the height of a standard table. The usual width of a raised bed is three to four feet. You can decide on the length of your raised bed, although four feet is generally considered the ideal length.

Once you have determined the height that you want and assembled your frame, you can start filling your raised bed with amended soil like the type used in flat beds or the soil that a container garden requires.

You can plant the same vegetables as you would in a flat bed and you can also include companion planting to help your garden grow optimally.

Advantages and Disadvantages of Raised Bed

The advantages of raised bed are a better condition of the soil (possibility of stepping on the plants is reduced to zero), improved water drainage, easy access (back friendly), and efficient weed and pest control.

The disadvantages are that the soil in a raised bed is warmer and requires more water, and it also requires time to make the frame.

In the end, raised bed is the better choice for someone who intends to grow more vegetables in the future and who has the needed space to do so.

Vegetables to Try

It is best to plant chard, spinach, kale, and other varieties of lettuce in the shaded part of your garden because they can tolerate such areas.

Plants like fennel, chives, basil, green beans, oregano, radish, garlic, squash, beets, peas, tomato, and most root crops love the sun. It is wise to place the said plants in an area that gets plenty of sunlight.

It does not take a genius to grow your own vegetables, but you need diligence and patience when growing them. Each plant will need to be watered every few days, and to receive enough sunlight. Caring for each plant by removing dead leaves, and getting rid of pests is also necessary.

Follow the steps in this guide and you will be enjoying your own home-grown vegetables in no time!

Conclusion

Thank you again for downloading this book!

I hope this book was able to help you learn more about vegetable gardening!

The next step is to put this information to use, and begin creating your own vegetable garden at home!

Also, don't forget to claim your FREE bonus e-book on how to grow tomatoes!
Download your copy HERE or click the link below:

http://bit.ly/1ODGQbJ

Finally, if you enjoyed this book, please take the time to share your thoughts and post a review on Amazon. It'd be greatly appreciated!

Thank you and good luck!

www.ingramcontent.com/pod-product-compliance
Lightning Source LLC
LaVergne TN
LVHW021747060526
838200LV00052B/3527